Fractions .
concepts

Author David Hudson
Editor Kathy Rogers

Table of Contents

Answer Keys

W5527 State Road 106, P.O. Box 800
Fort Atkinson, WI 53538

Equivalent Fractions Chart

1

$\frac{1}{2}$ | $\frac{1}{2}$

$\frac{1}{4}$ | $\frac{1}{4}$ | $\frac{1}{4}$ | $\frac{1}{4}$

$\frac{1}{8}$ | $\frac{1}{8}$ | $\frac{1}{8}$ | $\frac{1}{8}$ | $\frac{1}{8}$ | $\frac{1}{8}$ | $\frac{1}{8}$ | $\frac{1}{8}$

$\frac{1}{12}$ | $\frac{1}{12}$ | $\frac{1}{12}$ | $\frac{1}{12}$ | $\frac{1}{12}$ | $\frac{1}{12}$ | $\frac{1}{12}$ | $\frac{1}{12}$ | $\frac{1}{12}$ | $\frac{1}{12}$ | $\frac{1}{12}$ | $\frac{1}{12}$

1

$\frac{1}{3}$ | $\frac{1}{3}$ | $\frac{1}{3}$

$\frac{1}{6}$ | $\frac{1}{6}$ | $\frac{1}{6}$ | $\frac{1}{6}$ | $\frac{1}{6}$ | $\frac{1}{6}$

$\frac{1}{9}$ | $\frac{1}{9}$ | $\frac{1}{9}$ | $\frac{1}{9}$ | $\frac{1}{9}$ | $\frac{1}{9}$ | $\frac{1}{9}$ | $\frac{1}{9}$ | $\frac{1}{9}$

$\frac{1}{12}$ | $\frac{1}{12}$ | $\frac{1}{12}$ | $\frac{1}{12}$ | $\frac{1}{12}$ | $\frac{1}{12}$ | $\frac{1}{12}$ | $\frac{1}{12}$ | $\frac{1}{12}$ | $\frac{1}{12}$ | $\frac{1}{12}$ | $\frac{1}{12}$

1

$\frac{1}{5}$ | $\frac{1}{5}$ | $\frac{1}{5}$ | $\frac{1}{5}$ | $\frac{1}{5}$

$\frac{1}{10}$ | $\frac{1}{10}$ | $\frac{1}{10}$ | $\frac{1}{10}$ | $\frac{1}{10}$ | $\frac{1}{10}$ | $\frac{1}{10}$ | $\frac{1}{10}$ | $\frac{1}{10}$ | $\frac{1}{10}$

Beginning Fractions

A fraction represents one or more parts of a whole which has been divided into equal parts.

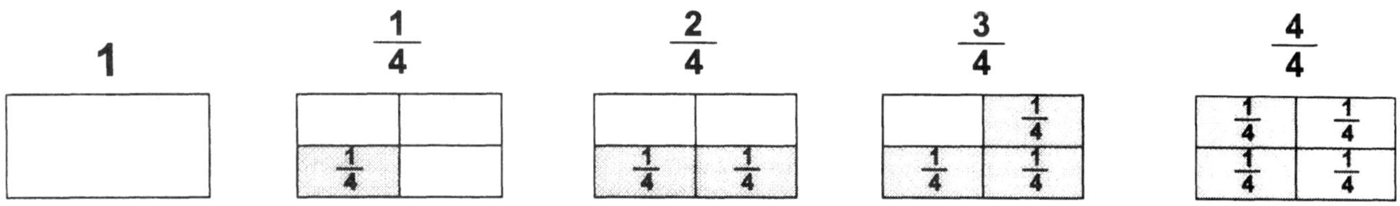

The bottom number of a fraction is called the **denominator**. It shows how many **equal** parts into which a whole is divided.

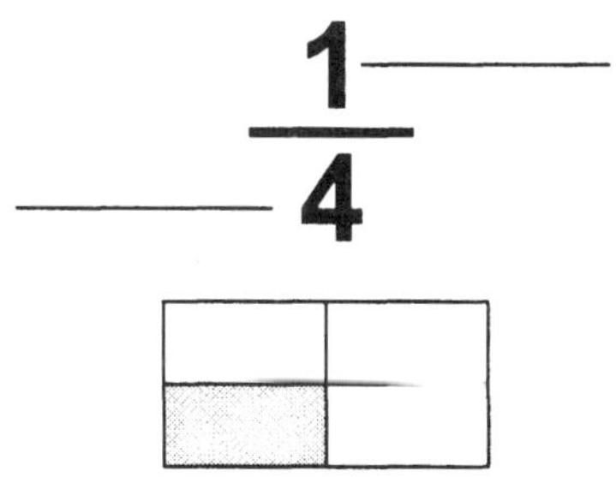

The top number is called the **numerator**. It shows how many of the equal parts the fraction represents.

Divide these rectangles into the number of equal parts shown and then write the fraction for one of the parts.

Example

Three parts $\frac{1}{3}$

Two parts ___

Five parts ___

Eight parts ___

Four parts ___

Six parts ___

Beginning Fractions

Divide the squares into the number of equal parts shown.
Shade one part.
Write the fraction for the shaded part and the fraction for the unshaded part.

Example

3 parts	Shaded	Unshaded
	$\frac{1}{3}$	$\frac{2}{3}$

4 parts	Shaded	Unshaded
	___	___

2 parts	Shaded	Unshaded
	___	___

5 parts	Shaded	Unshaded
	___	___

6 parts	Shaded	Unshaded
	___	___

3 parts	Shaded	Unshaded
	___	___

8 parts	Shaded	Unshaded
	___	___

9 parts	Shaded	Unshaded
	___	___

Beginning Fractions

Write the fraction for the shaded part of each shape.

Example

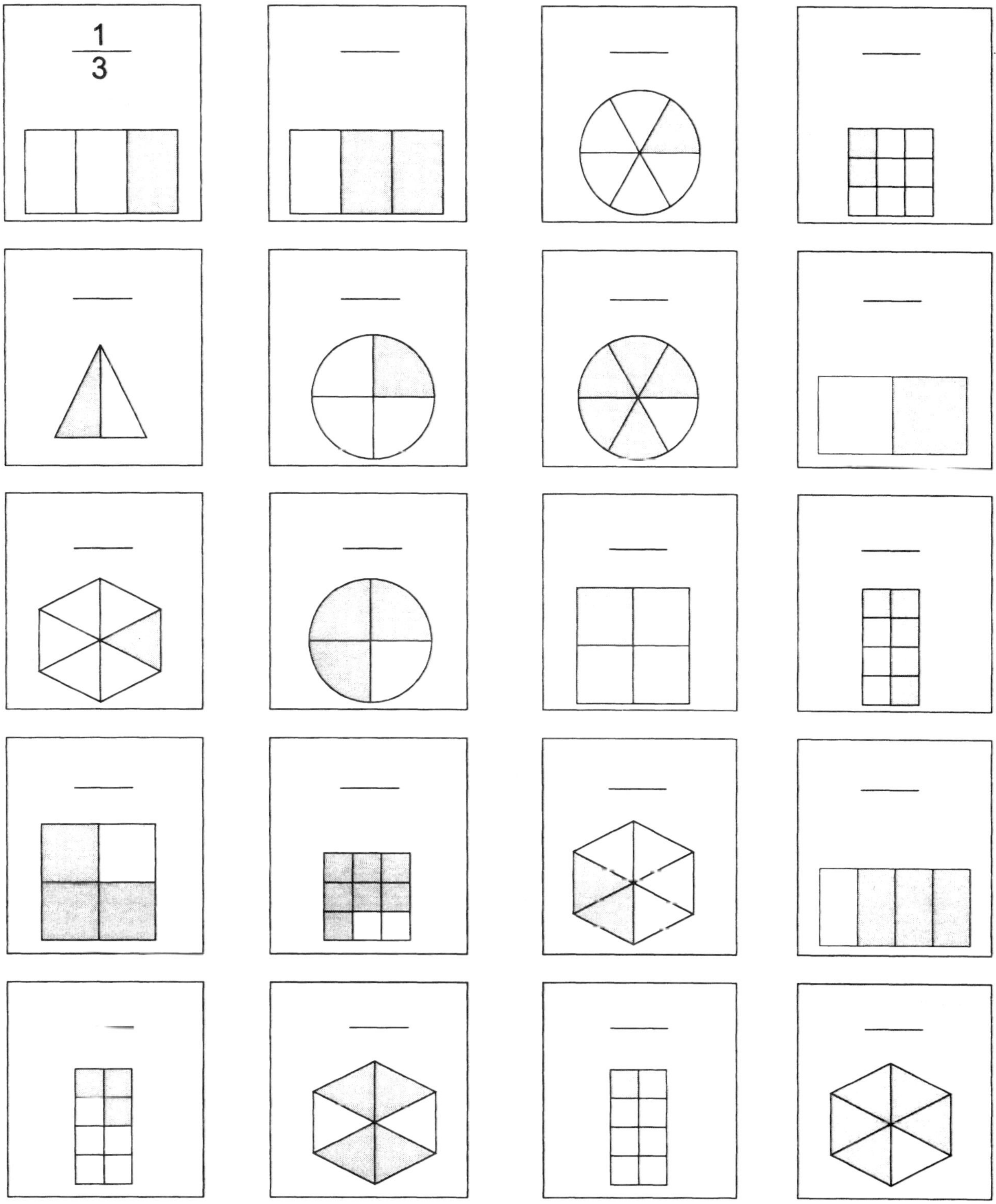

Beginning Fractions

Write the fractions for the shaded and unshaded parts of each shape.

Example

Shaded $\frac{1}{3}$ Unshaded $\frac{2}{3}$

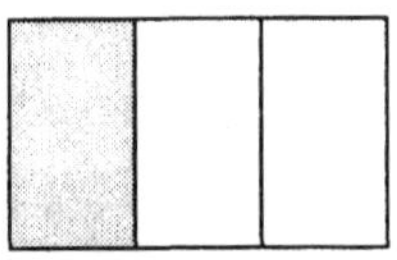

Shaded Unshaded

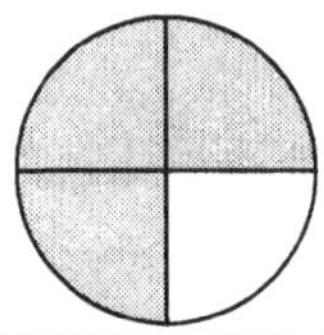

Shaded Unshaded

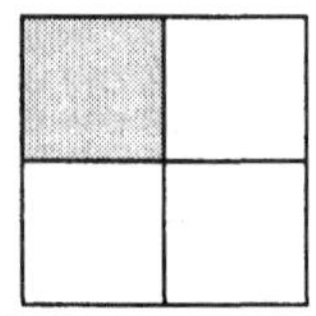

Shaded Unshaded

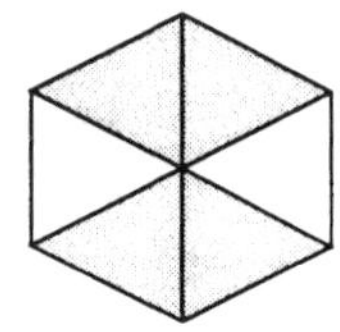

Shaded Unshaded

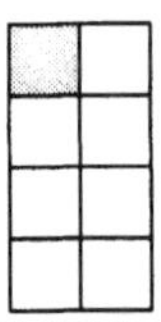

Shaded Unshaded

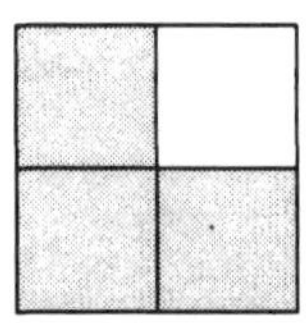

Shaded Unshaded

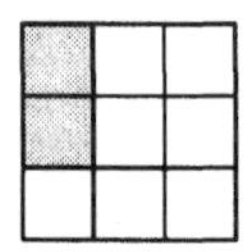

Shaded Unshaded

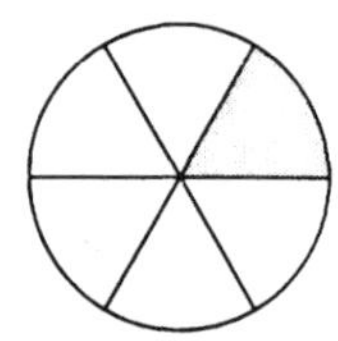

Shaded Unshaded

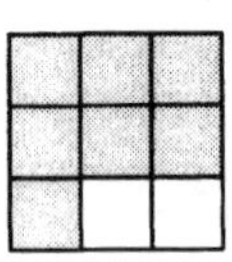

Shaded Unshaded

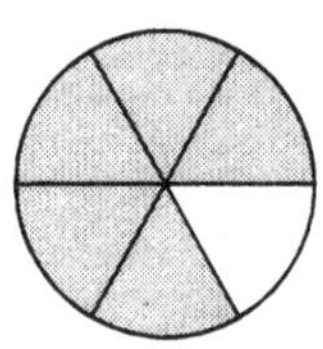

Shaded Unshaded

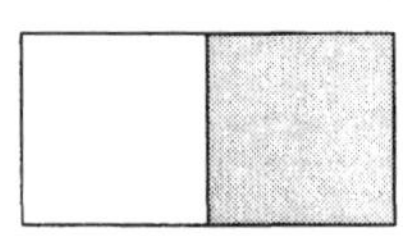

Shaded Unshaded

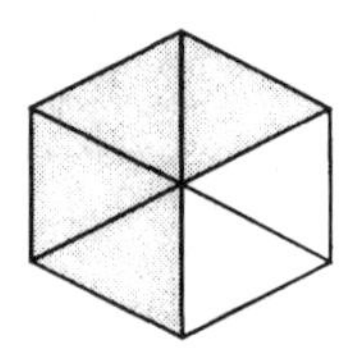

Shaded Unshaded

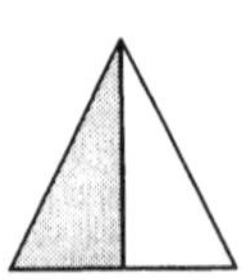

Shaded Unshaded

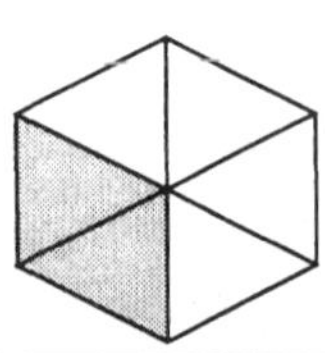

Shaded Unshaded

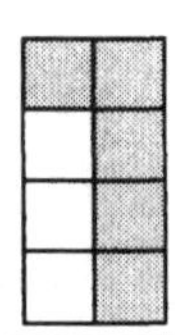

Shaded Unshaded

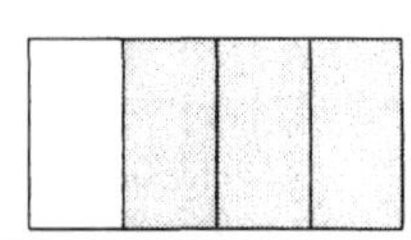

Beginning Fractions

Shade the parts of the shapes below as indicated by the fractions.

Example Example

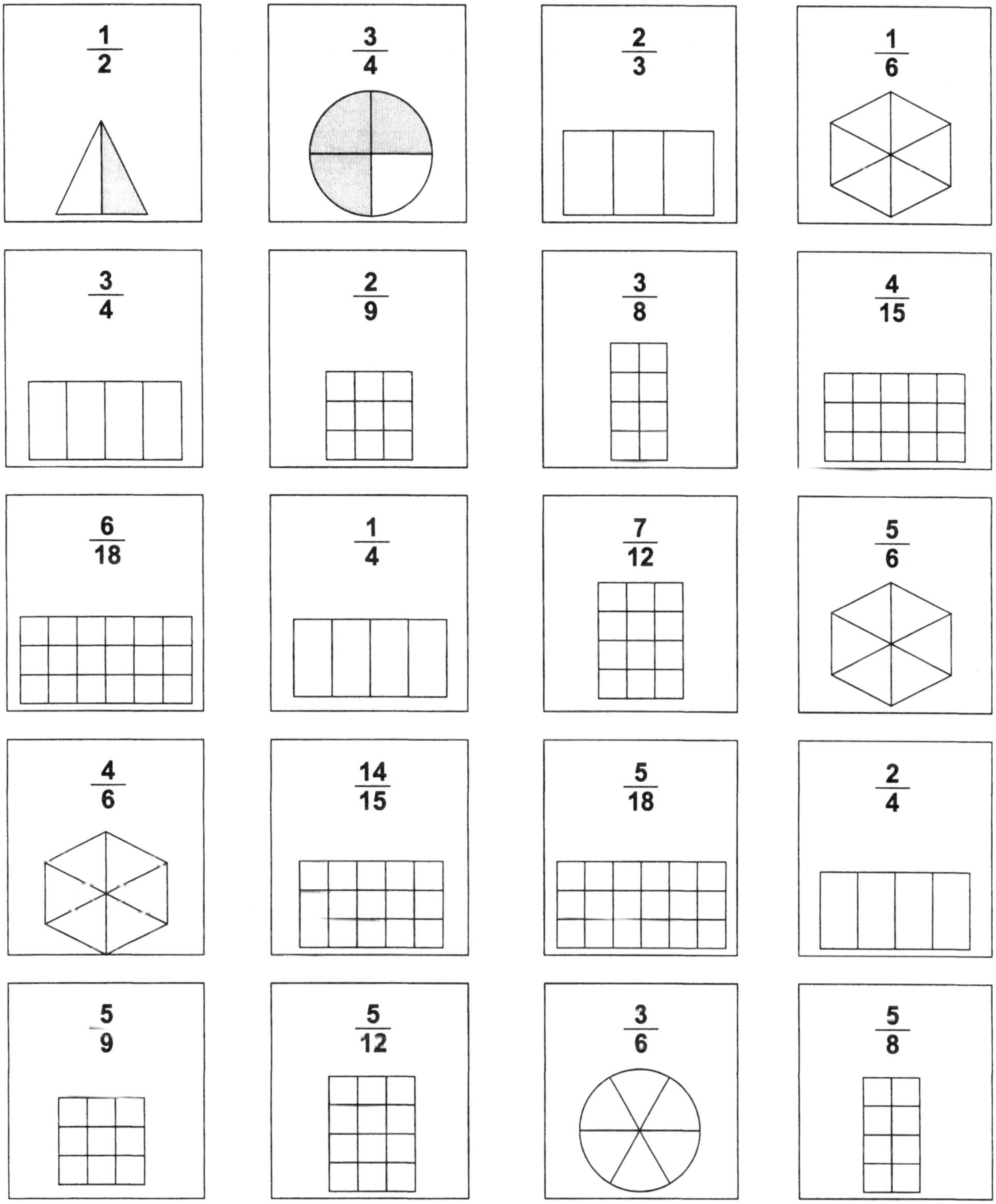

Beginning Fractions

Divide the shapes below and shade them as indicated by the fractions.

Example	Example		
$\frac{3}{4}$ 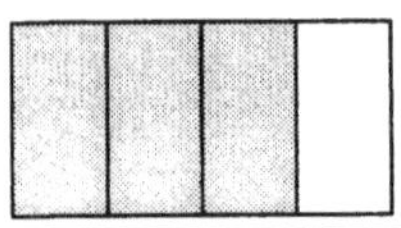	$\frac{5}{6}$ 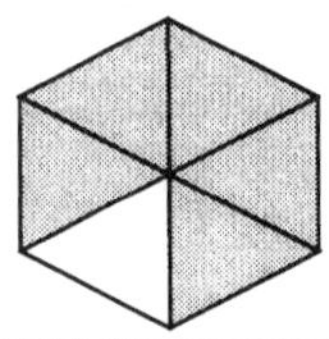	$\frac{1}{2}$	$\frac{1}{6}$
$\frac{3}{8}$	$\frac{2}{3}$	$\frac{3}{4}$	$\frac{5}{9}$
$\frac{4}{5}$	$\frac{2}{9}$	$\frac{7}{8}$	$\frac{1}{2}$
$\frac{5}{6}$	$\frac{3}{4}$	$\frac{2}{4}$	$\frac{1}{3}$
$\frac{4}{9}$	$\frac{2}{5}$	$\frac{4}{6}$	$\frac{3}{8}$

Beginning Fractions

A fraction can also represent one or more parts of a set (group of items).

1	$\frac{1}{4}$	$\frac{2}{4}$	$\frac{3}{4}$	$\frac{4}{4}$

Write the fraction which represents one part of each set below in words and in numbers.

Example

$\frac{1}{6}$

one sixth

______ ______

______ ______

______ ______

______ ______

______ ______

______ ______

______ ______

______ ______

______ ______

Beginning Fractions

Circle the part of each set represented by the fraction.

Example

$\frac{1}{4}$

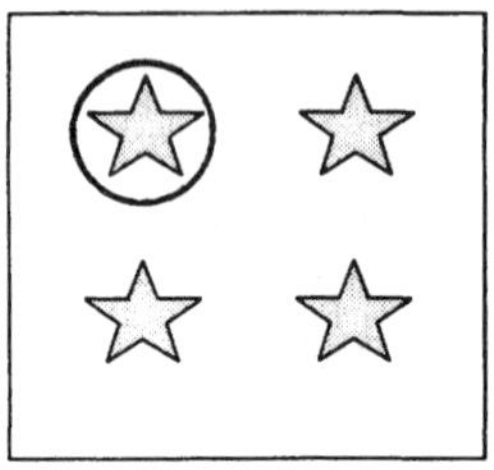

$\frac{2}{4}$

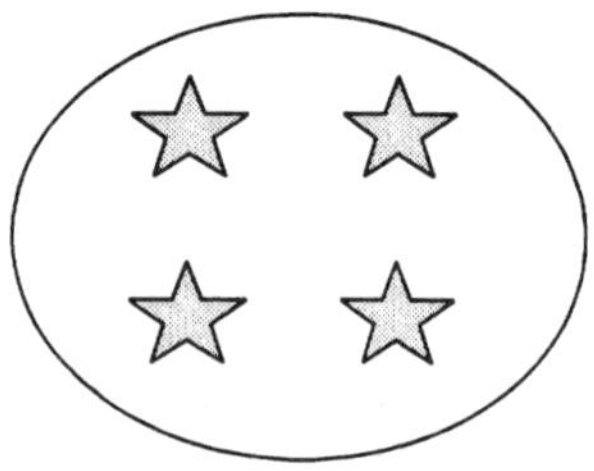

$\frac{3}{6}$

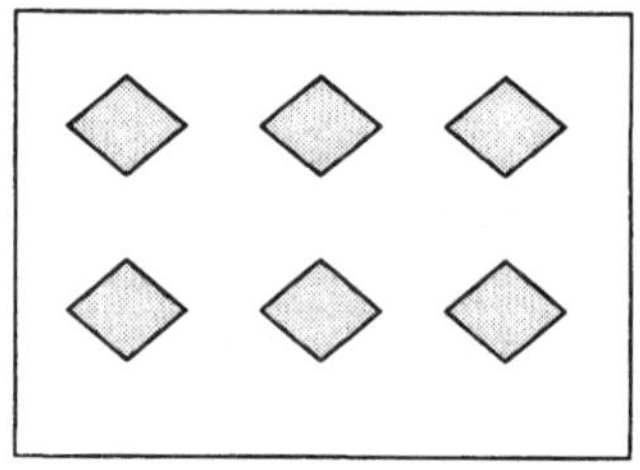

$\frac{5}{6}$

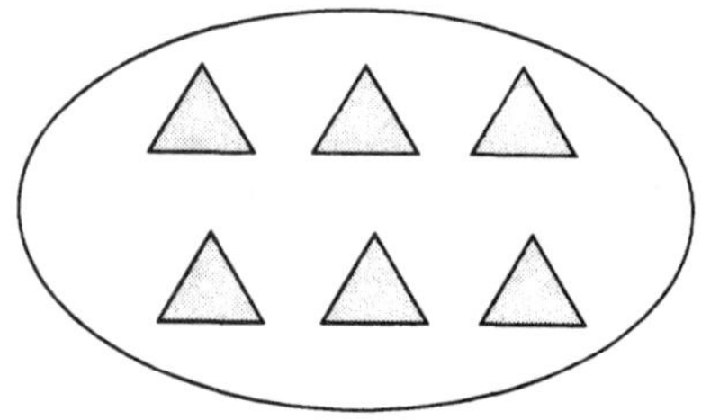

$\frac{1}{3}$

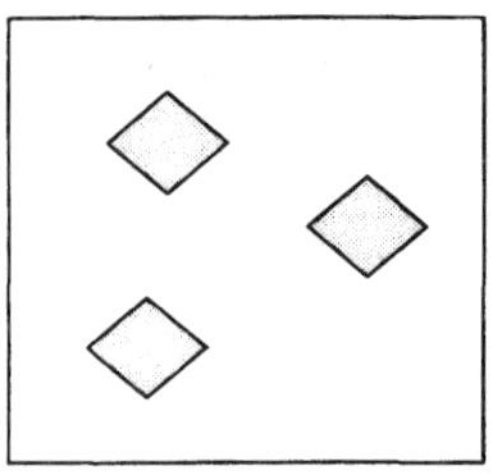

$\frac{1}{5}$

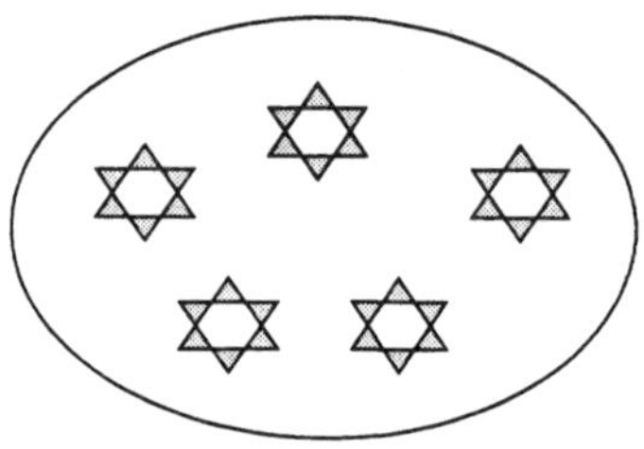

$\frac{3}{4}$

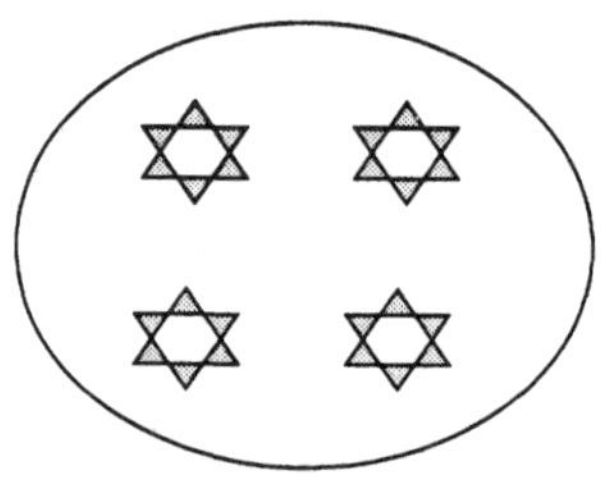

$\frac{2}{6}$

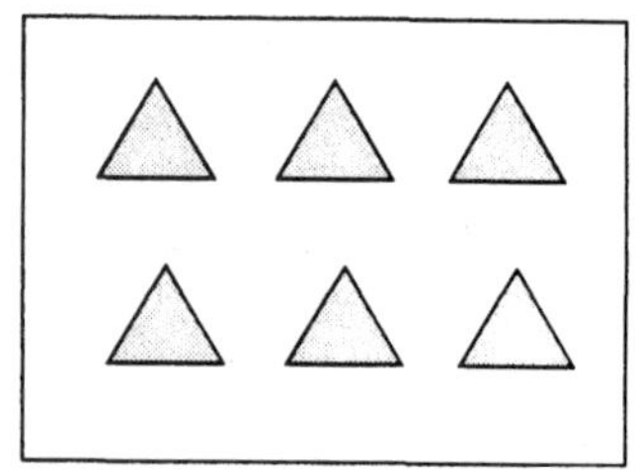

$\frac{1}{8}$

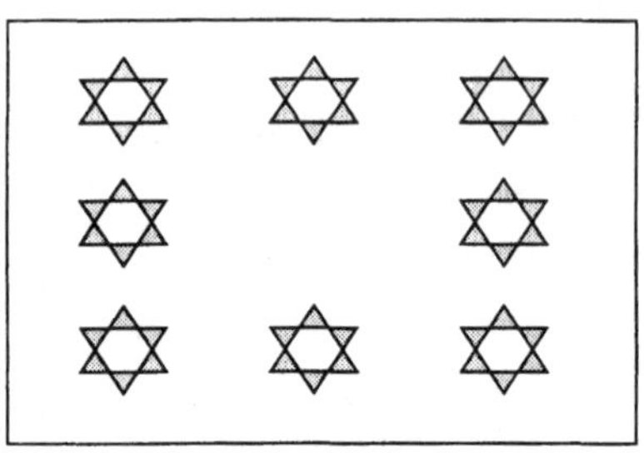

$\frac{4}{9}$

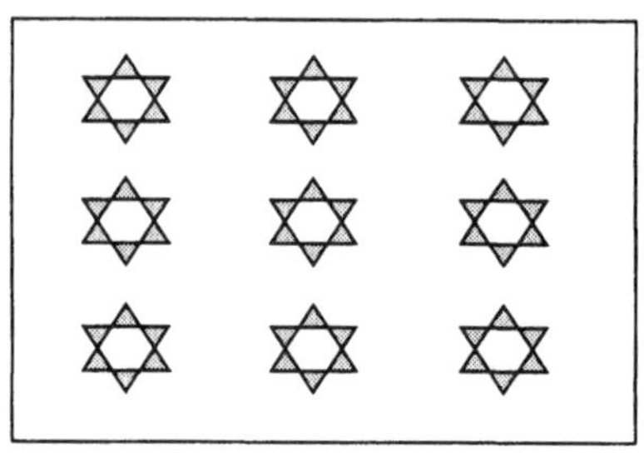

$\frac{7}{8}$

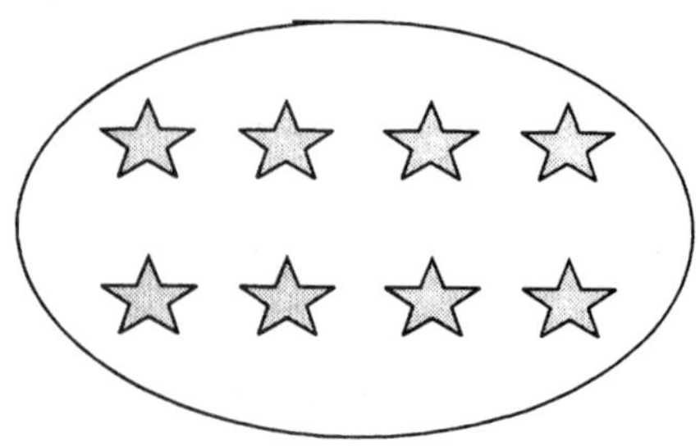

$\frac{4}{8}$

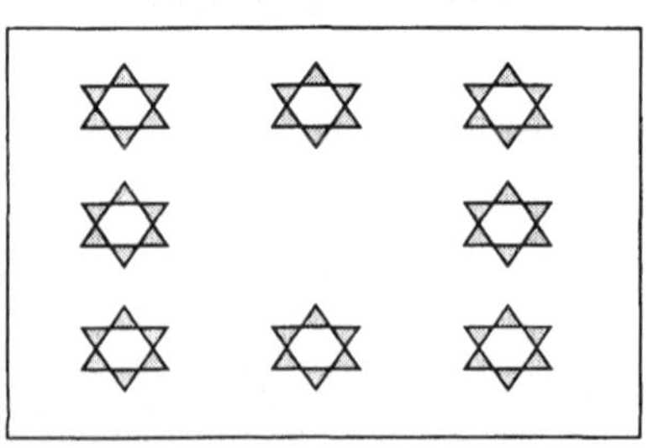

$\frac{2}{3}$

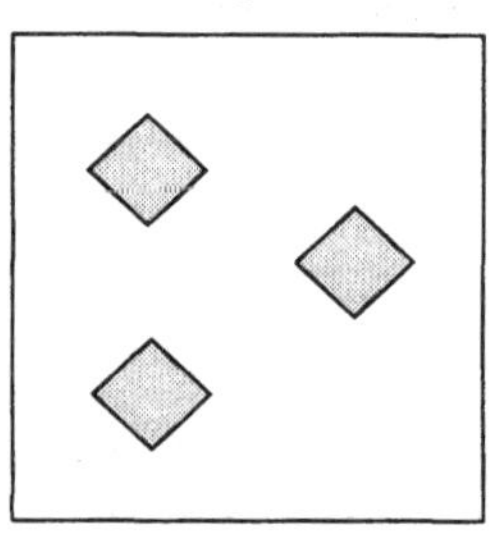

$\frac{3}{5}$

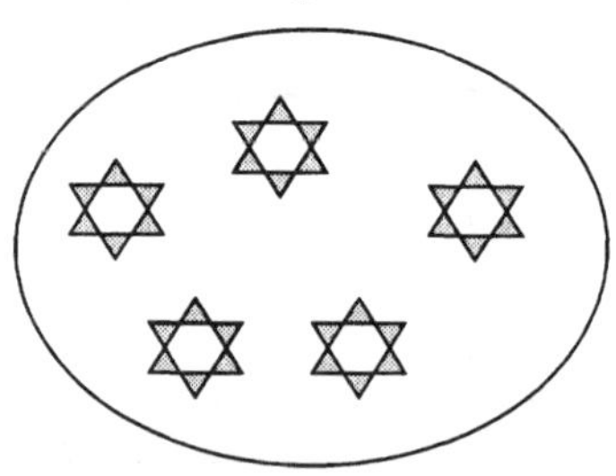

$\frac{4}{6}$

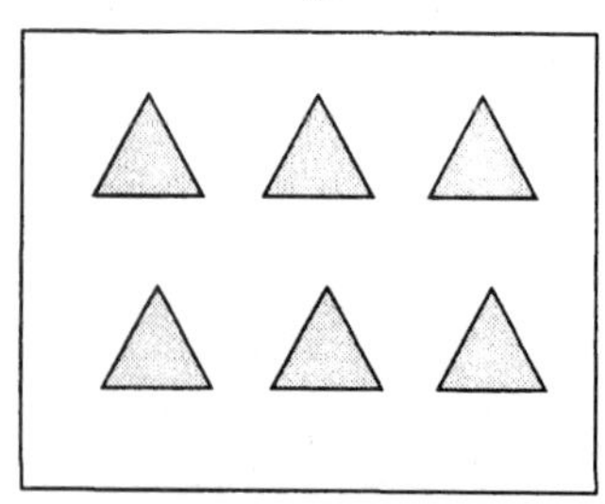

Parts of a Set

Beginning Fractions

Write the fraction for the shaded and unshaded stars in each set.

Example

Shaded $\frac{1}{4}$ Unshaded $\frac{3}{4}$

Shaded ___ Unshaded ___

Shaded ___ Unshaded ___

Shaded ___ Unshaded ___

Shaded ___ Unshaded ___

Shaded ___ Unshaded ___

Shaded ___ Unshaded ___

Shaded ___ Unshaded ___

Shaded ___ Unshaded ___

Shaded ___ Unshaded ___

Shaded ___ Unshaded ___

Shaded ___ Unshaded ___

Shaded ___ Unshaded ___

Shaded ___ Unshaded ___

Shaded ___ Unshaded ___

Beginning Fractions

When the numerator and denominator are the same, a fraction is equal to one.

$1 \text{ or } \frac{1}{1}$ = $\frac{4}{4}$ = $\frac{8}{8}$ = $\frac{16}{16}$

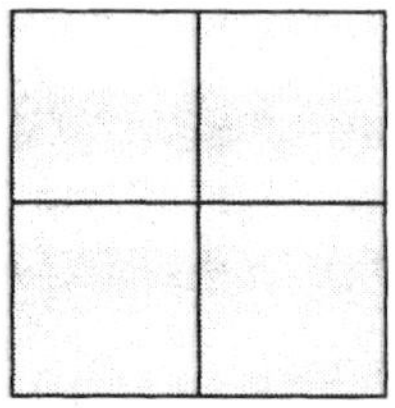
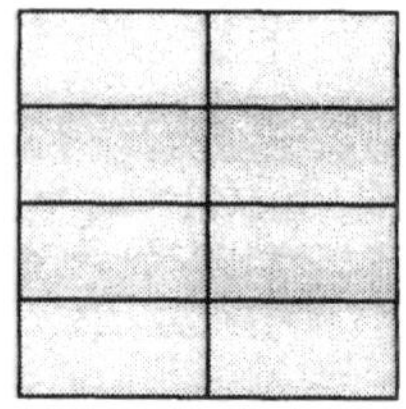
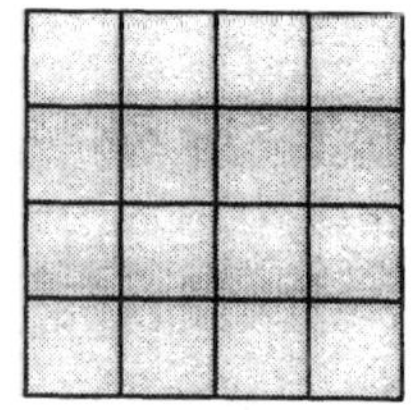

Write fractions equal to one for each of these shapes.

Example

$\frac{4}{4}$

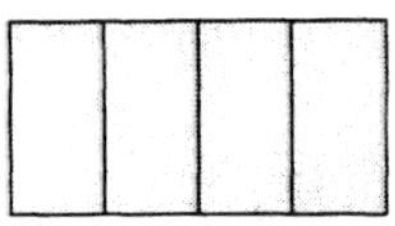

—

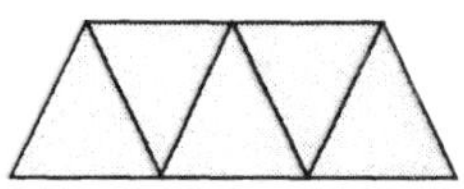

—

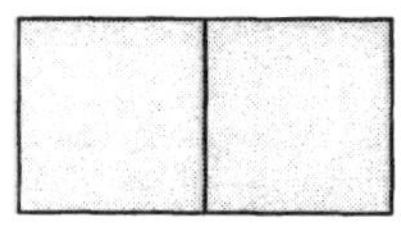

—

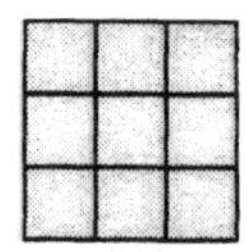

—

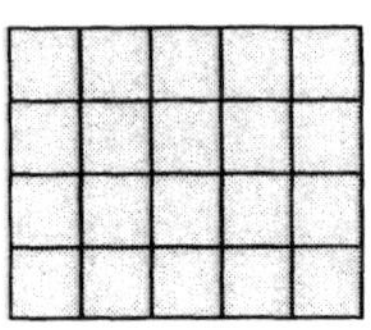

—

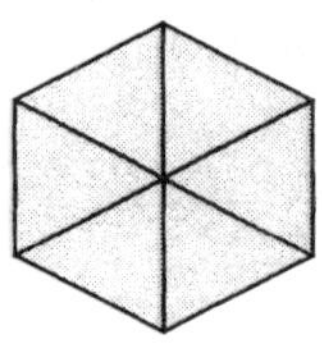

—

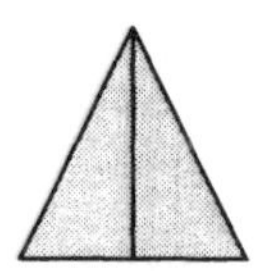

—

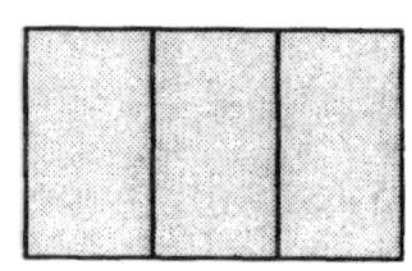

—

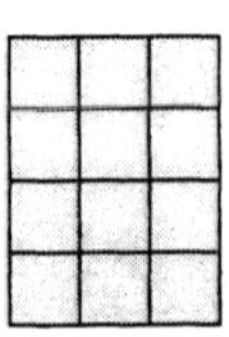

—

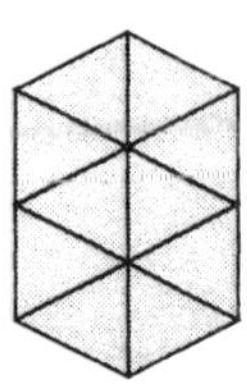

—

—

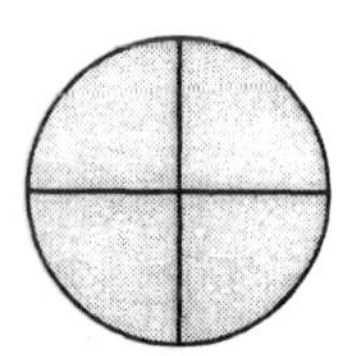

Beginning Fractions

When we compare numbers, we can use these symbols to represent which is larger.

$>$	means greater than	$8 > 6$
$=$	means equal to	$6 = 6$
$<$	means less than	$6 < 8$

Use symbols to compare these numbers.

Example

$8 > 6$ | 11 5 | 9 9 | 2 6 | 1 5 | 7 3

When comparing fractions with the same denominator, compare the numerator. The fraction with the larger numerator is larger.

$\frac{3}{4} > \frac{2}{4}$ $\frac{1}{4} < \frac{2}{4}$ $\frac{2}{4} = \frac{2}{4}$

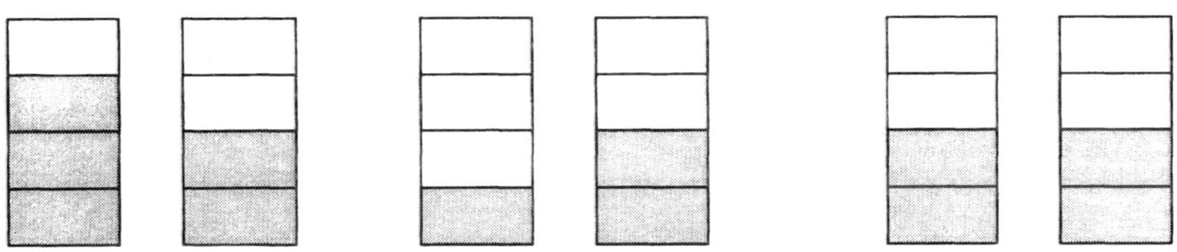

Compare these fractions.

Example

$\frac{2}{3} > \frac{1}{3}$

$\frac{7}{8}$ $\frac{7}{8}$

$\frac{3}{10}$ $\frac{7}{10}$

$\frac{7}{19}$ $\frac{5}{19}$

$\frac{5}{8}$ $\frac{7}{8}$

$\frac{1}{5}$ $\frac{3}{5}$

$\frac{8}{9}$ $\frac{5}{9}$

$\frac{2}{13}$ $\frac{11}{13}$

$\frac{1}{9}$ $\frac{1}{9}$

$\frac{5}{6}$ $\frac{2}{6}$

$\frac{1}{3}$ $\frac{1}{3}$

$\frac{2}{5}$ $\frac{2}{5}$

$\frac{1}{7}$ $\frac{3}{7}$

$\frac{4}{5}$ $\frac{3}{5}$

$\frac{2}{7}$ $\frac{4}{7}$

$\frac{16}{20}$ $\frac{17}{20}$

Beginning Fractions

When comparing fractions with the same numerator, compare the denominator. The fraction with the smaller denominator is larger.

$\frac{3}{4} > \frac{3}{6}$ $\frac{3}{6} < \frac{3}{4}$ $\frac{3}{6} = \frac{3}{6}$

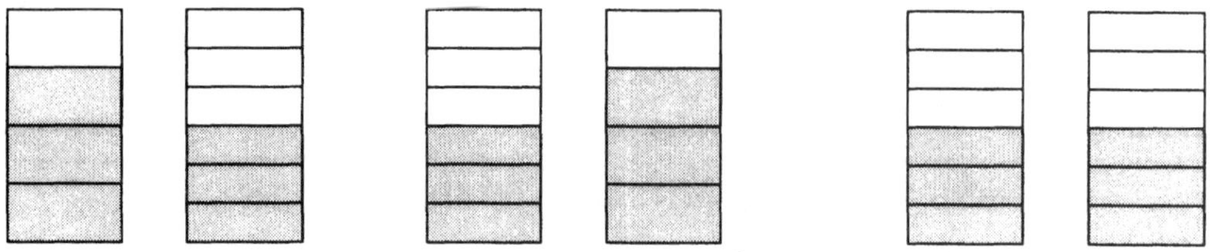

Compare these fractions.

Example			
$\frac{1}{3} > \frac{1}{6}$	$\frac{1}{8}$ $\frac{1}{6}$	$\frac{1}{9}$ $\frac{1}{3}$	$\frac{1}{4}$ $\frac{1}{7}$
$\frac{4}{5}$ $\frac{4}{8}$	$\frac{3}{4}$ $\frac{3}{5}$	$\frac{5}{6}$ $\frac{5}{7}$	$\frac{3}{5}$ $\frac{3}{5}$
$\frac{3}{10}$ $\frac{3}{5}$	$\frac{8}{9}$ $\frac{8}{15}$	$\frac{1}{3}$ $\frac{1}{3}$	$\frac{4}{7}$ $\frac{4}{9}$

Put these fractions in order from smallest to largest.

Example

$\frac{3}{8}$ $\frac{3}{4}$ $\frac{3}{14}$ $\frac{3}{9}$

$\frac{3}{14}$ $\frac{3}{9}$ $\frac{3}{8}$ $\frac{3}{4}$

$\frac{2}{7}$ $\frac{2}{5}$ $\frac{2}{19}$ $\frac{2}{8}$

___ ___ ___ ___

$\frac{4}{5}$ $\frac{4}{11}$ $\frac{4}{6}$ $\frac{4}{18}$

___ ___ ___ ___

$\frac{7}{9}$ $\frac{7}{18}$ $\frac{7}{10}$ $\frac{7}{8}$

___ ___ ___ ___

Beginning Fractions

Compare these fractions.

Example

$\frac{5}{6} > \frac{2}{6}$

$\frac{3}{5}$ $\frac{2}{5}$

$\frac{3}{5}$ $\frac{3}{10}$

$\frac{1}{6}$ $\frac{1}{3}$

$\frac{3}{5}$ $\frac{3}{8}$

$\frac{5}{8}$ $\frac{5}{6}$

$\frac{3}{4}$ $\frac{3}{4}$

$\frac{8}{9}$ $\frac{6}{9}$

$\frac{5}{8}$ $\frac{1}{8}$

$\frac{2}{7}$ $\frac{6}{7}$

$\frac{4}{9}$ $\frac{2}{9}$

$\frac{3}{7}$ $\frac{3}{6}$

$\frac{5}{8}$ $\frac{3}{8}$

$\frac{1}{3}$ $\frac{1}{9}$

$\frac{5}{6}$ $\frac{5}{6}$

$\frac{1}{7}$ $\frac{1}{4}$

$\frac{2}{5}$ $\frac{3}{5}$

$\frac{4}{9}$ $\frac{4}{9}$

$\frac{3}{7}$ $\frac{4}{7}$

$\frac{1}{4}$ $\frac{2}{4}$

Put these fractions in order from smallest to largest.

Example

$\frac{2}{3}$ $\frac{2}{5}$ $\frac{2}{9}$ $\frac{2}{4}$

$\frac{2}{9}$ $\frac{2}{5}$ $\frac{2}{4}$ $\frac{2}{3}$

$\frac{2}{9}$ $\frac{2}{3}$ $\frac{2}{11}$ $\frac{2}{7}$

___ ___ ___ ___

$\frac{4}{5}$ $\frac{3}{5}$ $\frac{1}{5}$ $\frac{5}{5}$

___ ___ ___ ___

$\frac{3}{9}$ $\frac{7}{9}$ $\frac{4}{9}$ $\frac{1}{9}$

___ ___ ___ ___

$\frac{8}{15}$ $\frac{8}{11}$ $\frac{8}{9}$ $\frac{8}{23}$

___ ___ ___ ___

$\frac{4}{9}$ $\frac{4}{11}$ $\frac{4}{7}$ $\frac{4}{6}$

___ ___ ___ ___

Beginning Fractions

The numbers that you multiply together to make a product are **factors** of the product.

1 x 6 = 6
2 x 3 = 6
1, 2, 3, and 6 are all factors of 6

Factors of 6	1	2	3	6						
Factors of 12	1	2	3	4	6	12				

Common factors are factors that are the same for two or more numbers. 1, 2, 3, and 6 are common factors of 6 and 12. The **greatest common factor** is the largest factor that is the same for two or more numbers. 6 is the greatest common factor of 6 and 12.

Find the greatest common factor of each pair of numbers below and circle it.

Example

12	1	2	3	4 (circled)	6	12				
16	1	2	4 (circled)	8	16					

27										
18										
28										
21										
24										
33										
56										
35										

Beginning Fractions

To reduce a fraction, divide both the numerator and denominator by the greatest common factor. A fraction is reduced to **lowest terms** when 1 is the only number which can be divided evenly into both the numerator and denominator.

The greatest common factor of 4 and 8 is 4

$$\frac{4 \div 4}{8 \div 4} = \frac{1}{2}$$

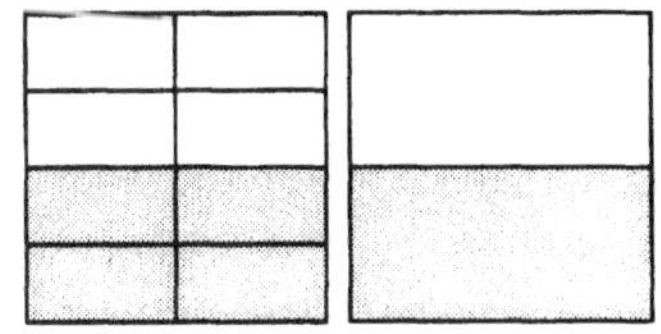

You can also reduce a fraction to lowest terms in more than one step.

Two steps

$$\frac{4 \div 2}{8 \div 2} = \frac{2}{4}$$

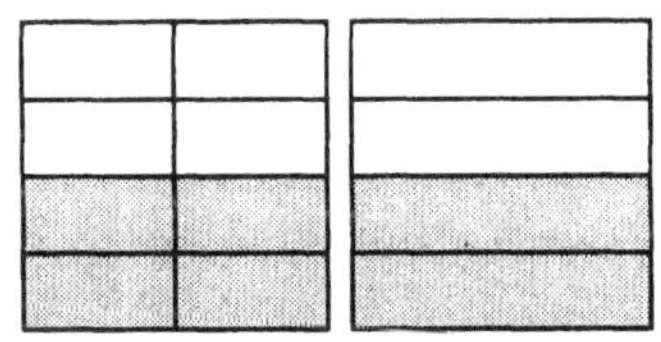

$$\frac{2 \div 2}{4 \div 2} = \frac{1}{2}$$

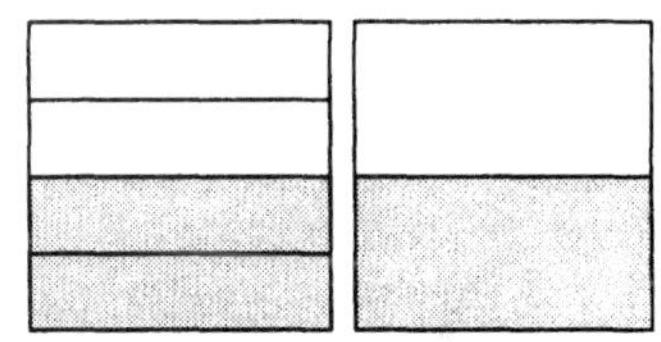

Reduce these fractions to lowest terms.

$\frac{9}{12}$	$\frac{8}{12}$	$\frac{10}{25}$
$\frac{32}{64}$	$\frac{20}{22}$	$\frac{6}{18}$
$\frac{8}{24}$	$\frac{3}{21}$	$\frac{6}{12}$
$\frac{18}{27}$	$\frac{16}{18}$	$\frac{11}{11}$

Beginning Fractions

Reduce these fractions to lowest terms.

$\frac{6}{8}$	$\frac{5}{10}$	$\frac{12}{15}$
$\frac{2}{4}$	$\frac{6}{15}$	$\frac{3}{9}$
$\frac{2}{8}$	$\frac{6}{9}$	$\frac{3}{6}$
$\frac{4}{10}$	$\frac{10}{12}$	$\frac{2}{6}$
$\frac{6}{14}$	$\frac{2}{16}$	$\frac{2}{12}$
$\frac{3}{15}$	$\frac{10}{20}$	$\frac{4}{12}$
$\frac{6}{6}$	$\frac{6}{10}$	$\frac{4}{8}$
$\frac{4}{6}$	$\frac{6}{18}$	$\frac{6}{15}$

Beginning Fractions

Reduce these fractions to lowest terms.

$\frac{14}{16}$ $\frac{9}{12}$ $\frac{5}{15}$

$\frac{12}{18}$ $\frac{10}{45}$ $\frac{50}{100}$

$\frac{10}{14}$ $\frac{24}{36}$ $\frac{6}{20}$

$\frac{9}{81}$ $\frac{8}{12}$ $\frac{10}{25}$

$\frac{32}{64}$ $\frac{20}{22}$ $\frac{6}{18}$

$\frac{15}{60}$ $\frac{6}{21}$ $\frac{10}{40}$

$\frac{6}{12}$ $\frac{16}{34}$ $\frac{32}{48}$

$\frac{5}{60}$ $\frac{12}{21}$ $\frac{11}{22}$

A fraction larger than one can be expressed as an **improper fraction** or as a **mixed number**. We sometimes use improper fractions during calculations. We usually change back to mixed numbers after a calculation is complete.

A **mixed number** is a combination of a whole number and a fraction.

An **improper fraction** is a fraction with a numerator larger than the denominator.

$$1\frac{1}{4} = \frac{5}{4}$$

1 and $\frac{1}{4}$

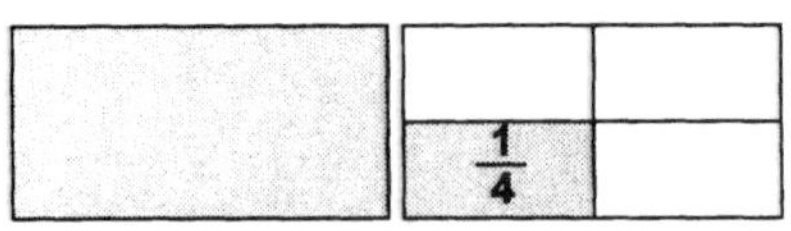

=

$\frac{4}{4}$ and $\frac{1}{4}$

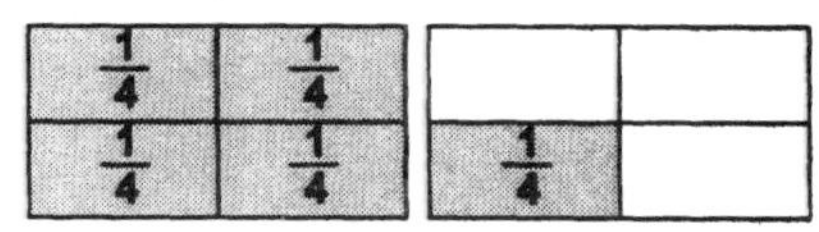

To change a mixed number to an improper fraction, first change the whole number to fraction form, then add it to the fractional part of the mixed number.

$$1\frac{2}{3} = \frac{3}{3} + \frac{2}{3} = \frac{5}{3}$$

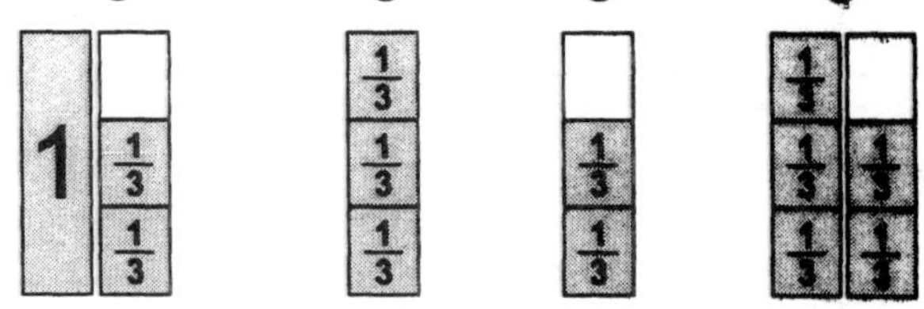

Change these mixed numbers to improper fractions.

$1\frac{1}{2}$	$1\frac{2}{5}$	$1\frac{3}{8}$
$1\frac{5}{6}$	$1\frac{1}{3}$	$1\frac{2}{7}$
$1\frac{3}{4}$	$1\frac{5}{12}$	$1\frac{7}{8}$

Beginning Fractions

You can also change a mixed number to an improper fraction by multiplying the denominator by the whole number. Then add the numerator. This sum becomes the numerator of the improper fraction.

$$3\frac{2}{3}$$

$$3 \times 3 = 9 + 2 = \frac{11}{3}$$

$$\frac{9}{3} + \frac{2}{3} = \frac{11}{3}$$

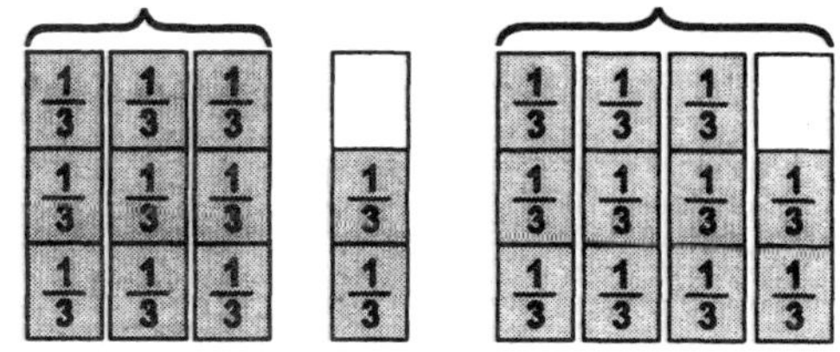

Change these mixed numbers to improper fractions.

$3\frac{2}{9}$	$2\frac{3}{16}$	$5\frac{3}{8}$
$4\frac{1}{4}$	$3\frac{5}{6}$	$2\frac{1}{3}$
$1\frac{5}{6}$	$2\frac{1}{5}$	$2\frac{3}{7}$
$3\frac{3}{5}$	$1\frac{7}{8}$	$4\frac{7}{10}$

Beginning Fractions

To change an improper fraction to a mixed number, first divide the numerator by the denominator. If there is a remainder, put the remainder over the denominator.

$$\frac{5}{3} = 3\overline{)5}^{\,1\text{ R}2} = 1\frac{2}{3}$$

$$\frac{5}{3} = 1 + \frac{2}{3} = 1\frac{2}{3}$$

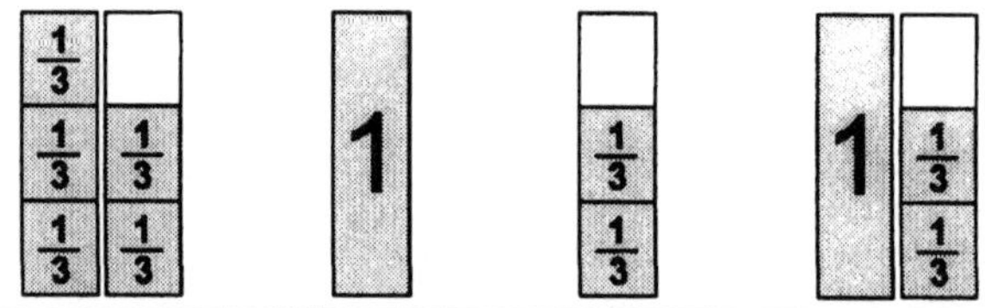

Change these improper fractions to mixed numbers or whole numbers.

$\frac{7}{5}$ $\frac{11}{7}$ $\frac{7}{4}$ $\frac{4}{3}$

$\frac{5}{2}$ $\frac{12}{7}$ $\frac{16}{3}$ $\frac{8}{3}$

$\frac{13}{5}$ $\frac{9}{4}$ $\frac{12}{3}$ $\frac{7}{6}$

$\frac{25}{24}$ $\frac{6}{5}$ $\frac{19}{2}$ $\frac{16}{4}$

$\frac{11}{5}$ $\frac{7}{2}$ $\frac{50}{5}$ $\frac{9}{7}$

Beginning Fractions

Change these improper fractions to mixed numbers or whole numbers.

$\frac{8}{5}$	$\frac{9}{7}$	$\frac{13}{4}$	$\frac{5}{3}$
$\frac{9}{5}$	$\frac{12}{7}$	$\frac{19}{3}$	$\frac{14}{3}$
$\frac{17}{4}$	$\frac{5}{4}$	$\frac{28}{3}$	$\frac{11}{6}$
$\frac{7}{2}$	$\frac{11}{7}$	$\frac{13}{9}$	$\frac{15}{3}$
$\frac{12}{5}$	$\frac{15}{4}$	$\frac{16}{4}$	$\frac{25}{6}$
$\frac{11}{3}$	$\frac{37}{5}$	$\frac{17}{2}$	$\frac{17}{4}$

Beginning Fractions

Equivalent fractions are fractions that are equal.

$\frac{1}{2} = \frac{2}{4} = \frac{4}{8}$

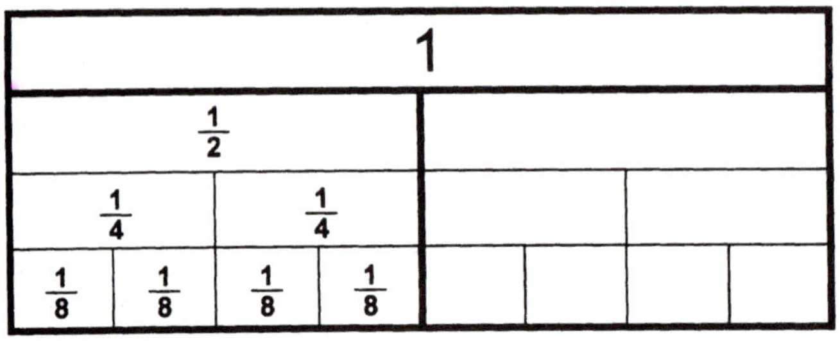

$\frac{1}{3} = \frac{2}{6} = \frac{3}{9}$

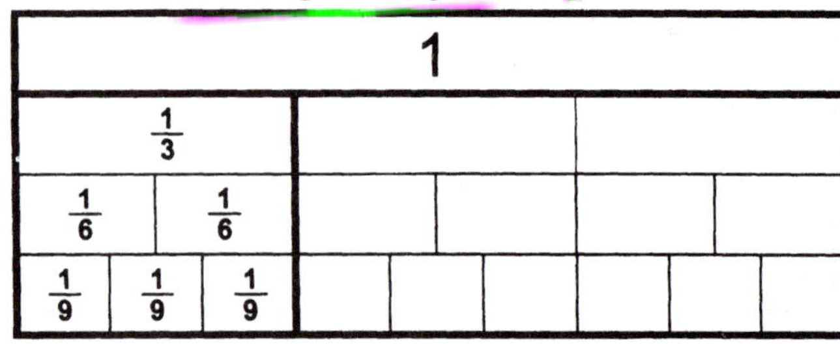

Write the fraction for the shaded part of the first rectangle. Then write the equivalent fractions represented in the second and third rectangles.

Example

$\frac{1}{2}$ = $\frac{2}{4}$ = $\frac{4}{8}$

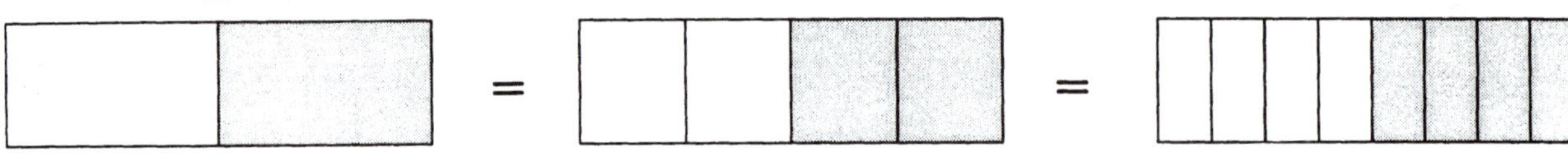

— = — = —

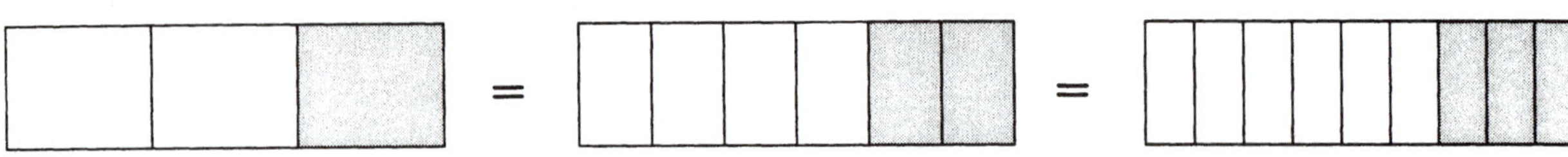

— = — = —

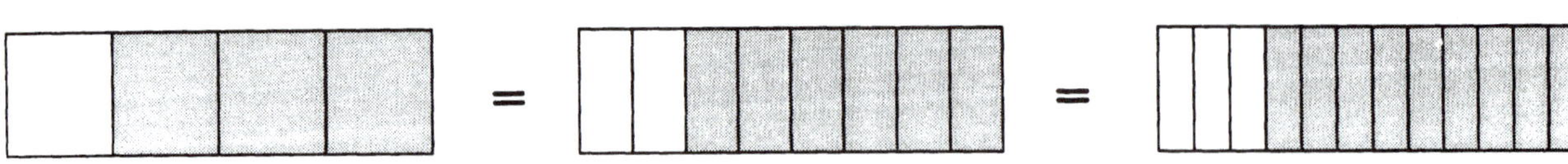

— = — = —

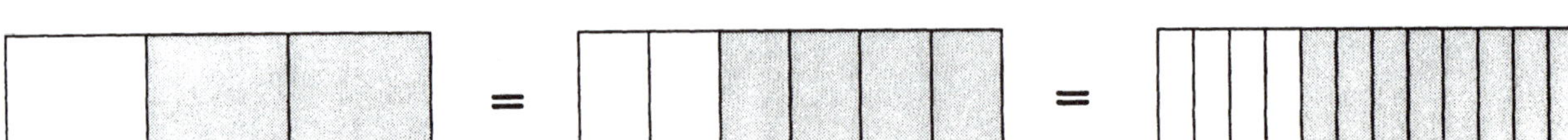

Beginning Fractions

To find an equivalent fraction, multiply both the numerator and denominator by the same number.

Examples

$$\frac{1 \times 2}{2 \times 2} = \frac{2}{4}$$

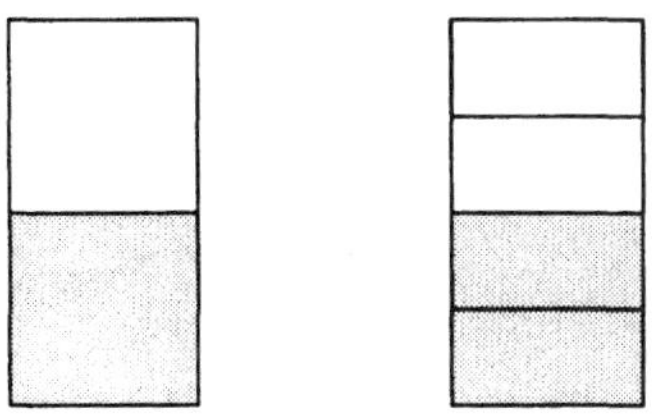

$$\frac{1 \times 4}{2 \times 4} = \frac{4}{8}$$

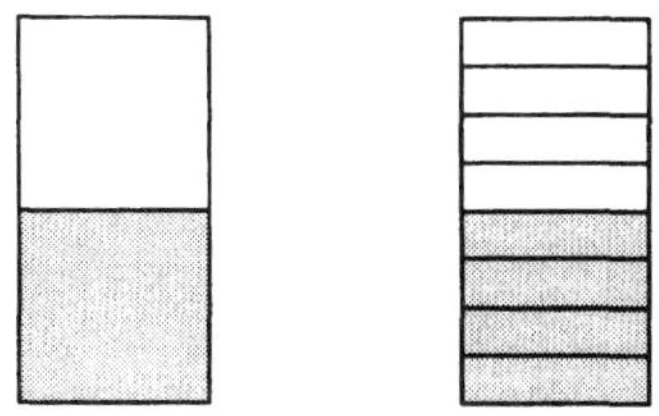

$$\frac{1 \times 3}{2 \times 3} = \frac{3}{6}$$

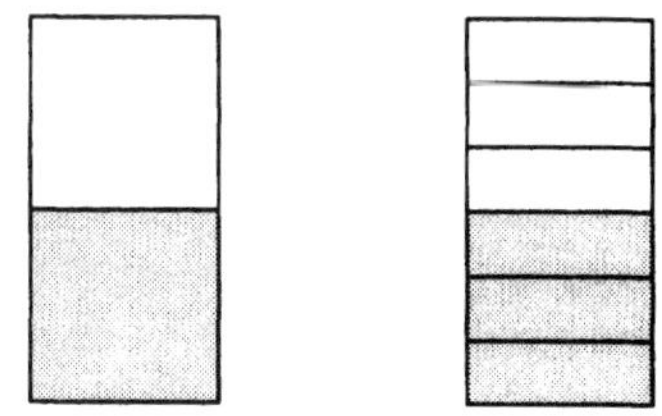

Make equivalent fractions.

Example

$$\frac{1 \times 3}{3 \times 3} = \frac{3}{9}$$

$\frac{1 \times \_}{3 \times \_} = \frac{\_}{12}$ $\quad$ $\frac{1 \times \_}{4 \times \_} = \frac{\_}{8}$

$\frac{1 \times \_}{2 \times \_} = \frac{\_}{8}$ $\quad$ $\frac{1 \times \_}{6 \times \_} = \frac{\_}{12}$ $\quad$ $\frac{1 \times \_}{5 \times \_} = \frac{\_}{15}$

$\frac{1 \times \_}{8 \times \_} = \frac{\_}{32}$ $\quad$ $\frac{1 \times \_}{5 \times \_} = \frac{\_}{30}$ $\quad$ $\frac{1 \times \_}{7 \times \_} = \frac{\_}{21}$

$\frac{2 \times \_}{3 \times \_} = \frac{\_}{9}$ $\quad$ $\frac{3 \times \_}{8 \times \_} = \frac{\_}{24}$ $\quad$ $\frac{4 \times \_}{5 \times \_} = \frac{\_}{20}$

$\frac{3 \times \_}{7 \times \_} = \frac{\_}{14}$ $\quad$ $\frac{2 \times \_}{9 \times \_} = \frac{\_}{18}$ $\quad$ $\frac{7 \times \_}{8 \times \_} = \frac{\_}{16}$

$\frac{5 \times \_}{7 \times \_} = \frac{\_}{21}$ $\quad$ $\frac{1 \times \_}{6 \times \_} = \frac{\_}{18}$ $\quad$ $\frac{7 \times \_}{9 \times \_} = \frac{\_}{27}$

Make equivalent fractions.

Example

$\frac{1 \times 2}{3 \times 2} = \frac{2}{6}$	$\frac{1 \times}{3 \times} = \frac{\quad}{9}$	$\frac{1 \times}{3 \times} = \frac{\quad}{36}$
$\frac{1 \times}{2 \times} = \frac{\quad}{4}$	$\frac{1 \times}{2 \times} = \frac{\quad}{6}$	$\frac{1 \times}{2 \times} = \frac{\quad}{8}$
$\frac{1 \times}{8 \times} = \frac{\quad}{24}$	$\frac{1 \times}{5 \times} = \frac{\quad}{30}$	$\frac{1 \times}{4 \times} = \frac{\quad}{12}$
$\frac{2 \times}{3 \times} = \frac{\quad}{6}$	$\frac{3 \times}{8 \times} = \frac{\quad}{16}$	$\frac{3 \times}{5 \times} = \frac{\quad}{10}$
$\frac{2 \times}{7 \times} = \frac{\quad}{14}$	$\frac{4 \times}{9 \times} = \frac{\quad}{18}$	$\frac{5 \times}{8 \times} = \frac{\quad}{16}$
$\frac{2 \times}{3 \times} = \frac{\quad}{9}$	$\frac{3 \times}{4 \times} = \frac{\quad}{12}$	$\frac{5 \times}{6 \times} = \frac{\quad}{30}$
$\frac{2 \times}{5 \times} = \frac{\quad}{10}$	$\frac{2 \times}{5 \times} = \frac{\quad}{15}$	$\frac{2 \times}{5 \times} = \frac{\quad}{20}$
$\frac{2 \times}{9 \times} = \frac{\quad}{27}$	$\frac{1 \times}{7 \times} = \frac{\quad}{21}$	$\frac{1 \times}{9 \times} = \frac{\quad}{18}$
$\frac{3 \times}{8 \times} = \frac{\quad}{24}$	$\frac{3 \times}{8 \times} = \frac{\quad}{32}$	$\frac{4 \times}{5 \times} = \frac{\quad}{20}$
$\frac{3 \times}{7 \times} = \frac{\quad}{14}$	$\frac{2 \times}{9 \times} = \frac{\quad}{18}$	$\frac{7 \times}{8 \times} = \frac{\quad}{24}$

Beginning Fractions

Write the fractions for the shaded and unshaded parts of each shape.

Shaded ___ **Unshaded** ___

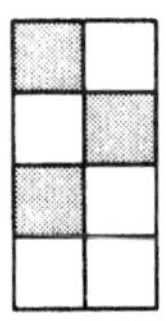

Shaded ___ **Unshaded** ___

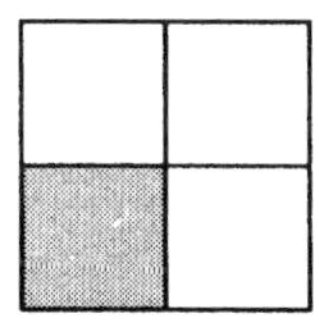

Shaded ___ **Unshaded** ___

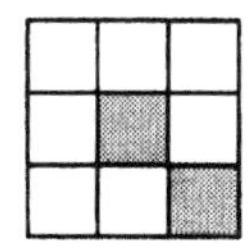

Shaded ___ **Unshaded** ___

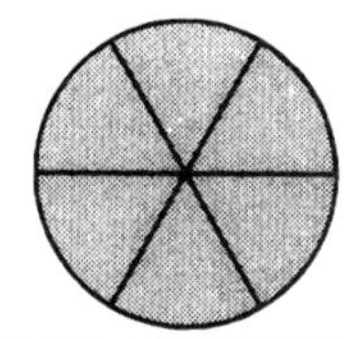

Write the fractions equivalent to 1 for these shapes.

___

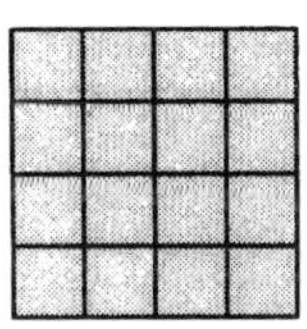

___

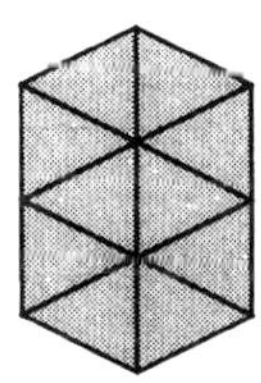

___

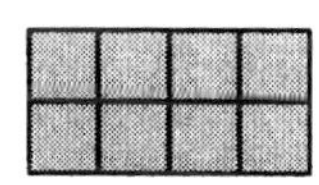

___

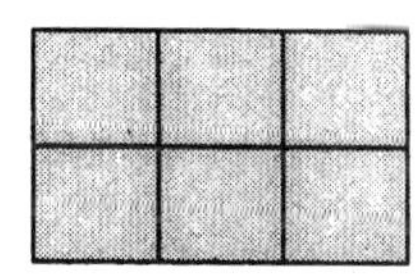

Find the greatest common factor for these pairs of numbers and circle it.

24										
21										
22										
33										
48										
36										

Put these fractions in order from smallest to largest.

$\frac{5}{19}$ $\frac{5}{7}$ $\frac{5}{9}$ $\frac{5}{23}$

___ ___ ___ ___

$\frac{3}{11}$ $\frac{9}{11}$ $\frac{7}{11}$ $\frac{2}{11}$

___ ___ ___ ___

Beginning Fractions

Reduce these fractions to lowest terms.

$\frac{10}{25}$ $\frac{18}{39}$ $\frac{14}{42}$

$\frac{32}{72}$ $\frac{8}{56}$ $\frac{9}{12}$

$\frac{8}{32}$ $\frac{6}{21}$ $\frac{44}{84}$

Change these mixed numbers to improper fractions.

$4\frac{1}{2}$ $2\frac{5}{11}$ $6\frac{5}{8}$

Change these improper fractions to mixed numbers reduced to lowest terms.

$\frac{75}{8}$ $\frac{17}{2}$ $\frac{33}{9}$ $\frac{26}{3}$

Make equivalent fractions.

$\frac{2}{3}\,\frac{x\ 3}{x\ 3} = \frac{\quad}{9}$ $\frac{1}{9}\,\frac{x}{x} = \frac{\quad}{81}$ $\frac{3}{4}\,\frac{x}{x} = \frac{\quad}{8}$

$\frac{4}{5}\,\frac{x}{x} = \frac{\quad}{20}$ $\frac{5}{6}\,\frac{x}{x} = \frac{\quad}{18}$ $\frac{3}{11}\,\frac{x}{x} = \frac{\quad}{66}$

$\frac{3}{7}\,\frac{x}{x} = \frac{\quad}{28}$ $\frac{4}{9}\,\frac{x}{x} = \frac{\quad}{27}$ $\frac{2}{7}\,\frac{x}{x} = \frac{\quad}{21}$

Answers
Pages 3 - 9

Beginning Fractions

Page 3

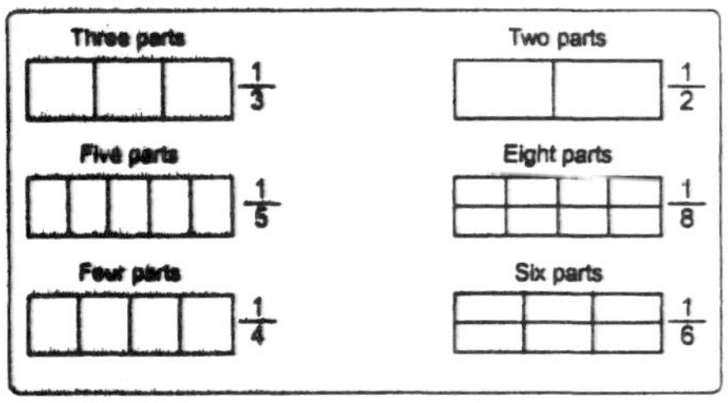

Page 4

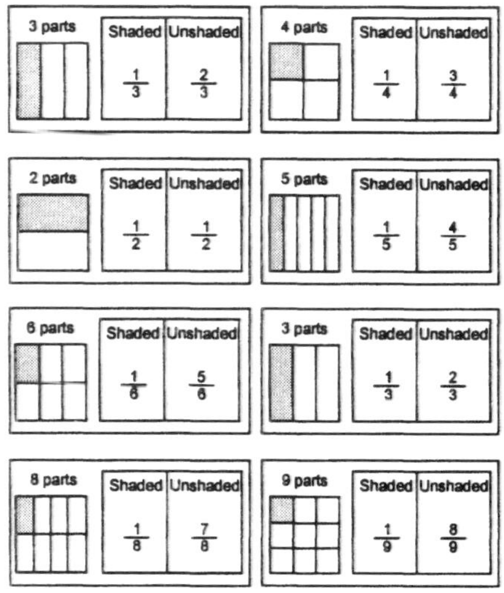

Page 5

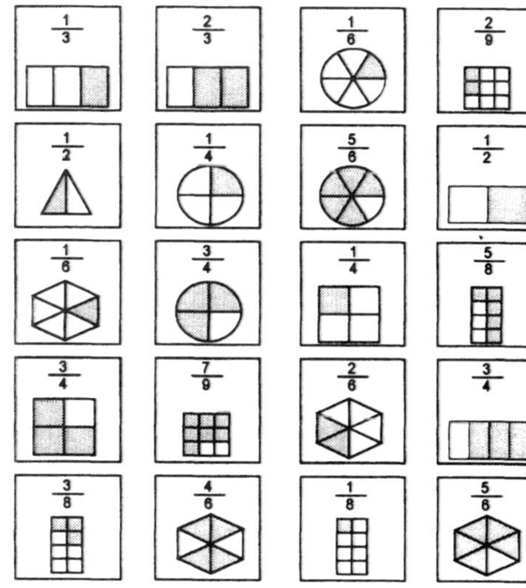

Page 6

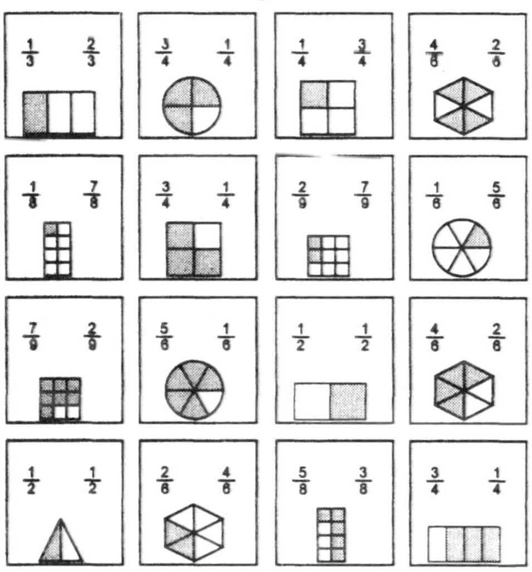

Page 7

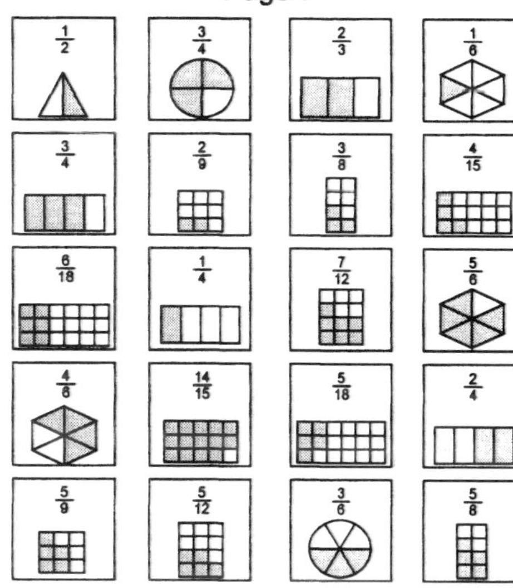

Page 8

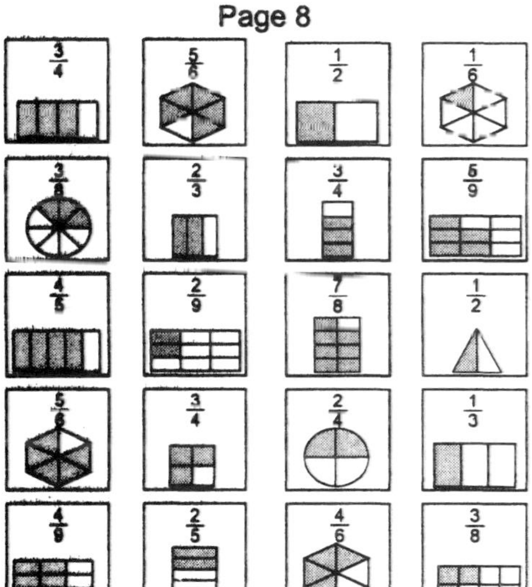

Page 9

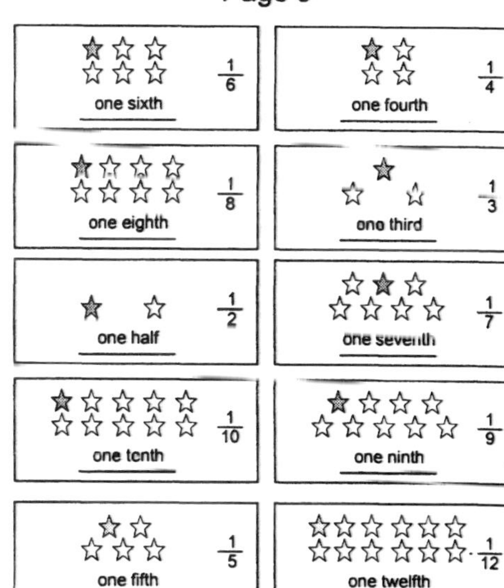

Beginning Fractions

Page 10

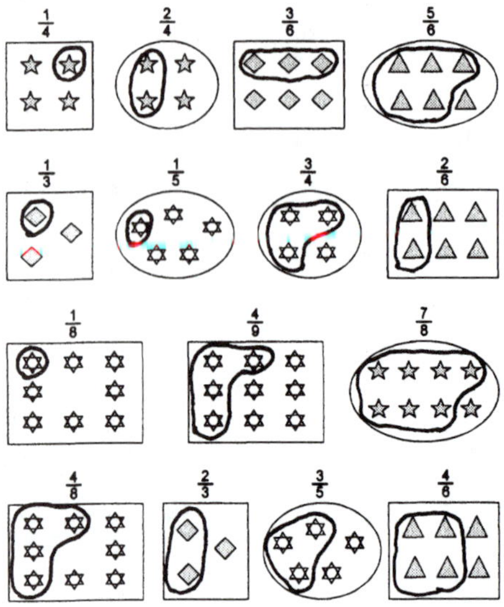

Page 11

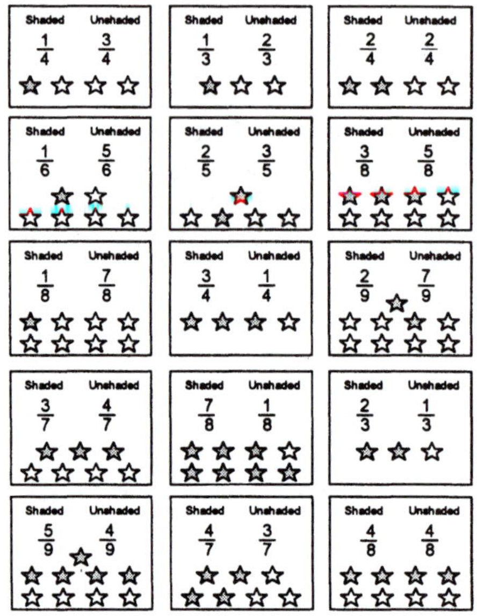

Page 12

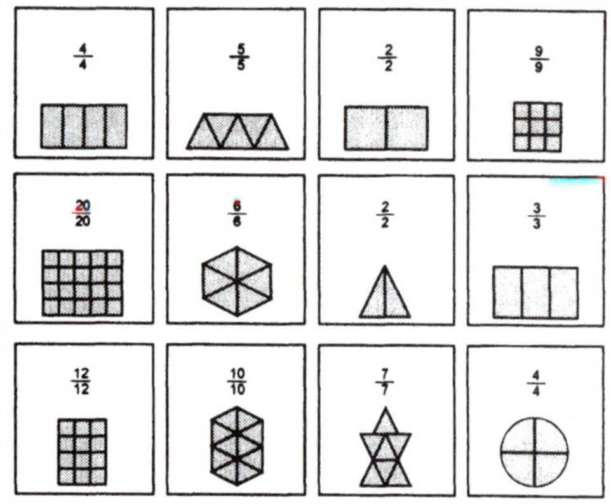

Page 13

$8 > 6$ $11 > 5$ $9 = 9$ $2 < 6$ $1 < 5$ $7 > 3$

$\frac{2}{3} > \frac{1}{3}$, $\frac{7}{8} = \frac{7}{8}$, $\frac{3}{10} < \frac{7}{10}$, $\frac{7}{19} > \frac{5}{19}$

$\frac{5}{8} < \frac{7}{8}$, $\frac{1}{5} < \frac{3}{5}$, $\frac{8}{9} > \frac{5}{9}$, $\frac{2}{13} < \frac{11}{13}$

$\frac{1}{9} = \frac{1}{9}$, $\frac{5}{6} > \frac{2}{6}$, $\frac{1}{3} = \frac{1}{3}$, $\frac{2}{5} = \frac{2}{5}$

$\frac{1}{7} < \frac{3}{7}$, $\frac{4}{5} > \frac{3}{5}$, $\frac{2}{7} < \frac{4}{7}$, $\frac{16}{20} < \frac{17}{20}$

Page 14

$\frac{1}{3} > \frac{1}{6}$, $\frac{4}{5} > \frac{4}{8}$, $\frac{3}{10} < \frac{3}{5}$

$\frac{1}{8} < \frac{1}{6}$, $\frac{3}{4} > \frac{3}{5}$, $\frac{8}{9} > \frac{8}{15}$

$\frac{1}{9} < \frac{1}{3}$, $\frac{5}{6} > \frac{5}{7}$, $\frac{1}{3} = \frac{1}{3}$

$\frac{1}{4} > \frac{1}{7}$, $\frac{3}{5} = \frac{3}{5}$, $\frac{4}{7} > \frac{4}{9}$

$\frac{3}{14}$ $\frac{3}{9}$ $\frac{3}{8}$ $\frac{3}{4}$

$\frac{2}{19}$ $\frac{2}{8}$ $\frac{2}{7}$ $\frac{2}{5}$

$\frac{4}{18}$ $\frac{4}{11}$ $\frac{4}{6}$ $\frac{4}{5}$

$\frac{7}{18}$ $\frac{7}{10}$ $\frac{7}{9}$ $\frac{7}{8}$

Page 15

$\frac{5}{6} > \frac{2}{6}$, $\frac{3}{5} > \frac{2}{5}$, $\frac{3}{5} > \frac{3}{10}$, $\frac{1}{6} < \frac{1}{3}$, $\frac{3}{5} > \frac{3}{8}$

$\frac{5}{8} < \frac{5}{6}$, $\frac{3}{4} = \frac{3}{4}$, $\frac{8}{9} > \frac{6}{9}$, $\frac{5}{8} > \frac{1}{8}$, $\frac{2}{7} < \frac{6}{7}$

$\frac{4}{9} > \frac{2}{9}$, $\frac{3}{7} < \frac{3}{6}$, $\frac{5}{8} > \frac{3}{8}$, $\frac{1}{3} > \frac{1}{9}$, $\frac{5}{6} = \frac{5}{6}$

$\frac{1}{7} < \frac{1}{4}$, $\frac{2}{5} < \frac{3}{5}$, $\frac{4}{9} = \frac{4}{9}$, $\frac{3}{7} < \frac{4}{7}$, $\frac{1}{4} < \frac{2}{4}$

$\frac{2}{9}$ $\frac{2}{5}$ $\frac{2}{4}$ $\frac{2}{3}$

$\frac{1}{5}$ $\frac{3}{5}$ $\frac{4}{5}$ $\frac{5}{5}$

$\frac{8}{23}$ $\frac{8}{15}$ $\frac{8}{11}$ $\frac{8}{9}$

$\frac{2}{11}$ $\frac{2}{9}$ $\frac{2}{7}$ $\frac{2}{3}$

$\frac{1}{9}$ $\frac{3}{9}$ $\frac{4}{9}$ $\frac{7}{9}$

$\frac{4}{11}$ $\frac{4}{9}$ $\frac{4}{7}$ $\frac{4}{6}$

Page 16

12	1	2	3	4	6	12				
16	1	2	4	8	16					
27	1	3	9							
18	1	2	3	6	9					
28	1	2	4	7						
21	1	3	7							
24	1	2	3							
33	1	3								
56	1	2	4	7						
35	1	5	7							

Answers
Pages 17 - 22

Beginning Fractions

Page 17

$\frac{3}{4}$	$\frac{2}{3}$	$\frac{2}{5}$
$\frac{1}{2}$	$\frac{10}{11}$	$\frac{1}{3}$
$\frac{1}{3}$	$\frac{1}{7}$	$\frac{1}{2}$
$\frac{2}{3}$	$\frac{8}{9}$	1

Page 18

$\frac{3}{4}$	$\frac{1}{2}$	$\frac{4}{5}$
$\frac{1}{2}$	$\frac{2}{5}$	$\frac{1}{3}$
$\frac{1}{4}$	$\frac{2}{3}$	$\frac{1}{2}$
$\frac{2}{5}$	$\frac{5}{6}$	$\frac{1}{3}$
$\frac{3}{7}$	$\frac{1}{8}$	$\frac{1}{6}$
$\frac{1}{5}$	$\frac{1}{2}$	$\frac{1}{3}$
1	$\frac{3}{5}$	$\frac{1}{2}$
$\frac{2}{3}$	$\frac{1}{3}$	$\frac{2}{5}$

Page 19

$\frac{7}{8}$	$\frac{3}{4}$	$\frac{1}{3}$
$\frac{2}{3}$	$\frac{2}{9}$	$\frac{1}{2}$
$\frac{5}{7}$	$\frac{2}{3}$	$\frac{3}{10}$
$\frac{1}{9}$	$\frac{2}{3}$	$\frac{2}{5}$
$\frac{1}{2}$	$\frac{10}{11}$	$\frac{1}{3}$
$\frac{1}{4}$	$\frac{2}{7}$	$\frac{1}{4}$
$\frac{1}{2}$	$\frac{8}{17}$	$\frac{2}{3}$
$\frac{1}{12}$	$\frac{4}{7}$	$\frac{1}{2}$

Page 20

$\frac{3}{2}$	$\frac{7}{5}$	$\frac{11}{8}$
$\frac{11}{6}$	$\frac{4}{3}$	$\frac{9}{7}$
$\frac{7}{4}$	$\frac{17}{12}$	$\frac{15}{8}$

Page 21

$\frac{29}{9}$	$\frac{35}{16}$	$\frac{43}{8}$
$\frac{17}{4}$	$\frac{23}{6}$	$\frac{7}{3}$
$\frac{11}{6}$	$\frac{11}{5}$	$\frac{17}{7}$
$\frac{18}{5}$	$\frac{15}{8}$	$\frac{47}{10}$

Page 22

$1\frac{2}{5}$	$1\frac{4}{7}$	$1\frac{3}{4}$	$1\frac{1}{3}$
$2\frac{1}{2}$	$1\frac{5}{7}$	$5\frac{1}{3}$	$2\frac{2}{3}$
$2\frac{3}{5}$	$2\frac{1}{4}$	4	$1\frac{1}{6}$
$1\frac{1}{24}$	$1\frac{1}{5}$	$9\frac{1}{2}$	4
$2\frac{1}{5}$	$3\frac{1}{2}$	10	$1\frac{2}{7}$

Beginning Fractions

Page 23

$1\frac{3}{5}$	$1\frac{2}{7}$	$3\frac{1}{4}$	$1\frac{2}{3}$
$1\frac{4}{5}$	$1\frac{5}{7}$	$6\frac{1}{3}$	$4\frac{2}{3}$
$4\frac{1}{4}$	$1\frac{1}{4}$	$9\frac{1}{3}$	$1\frac{5}{6}$
$3\frac{1}{2}$	$1\frac{4}{7}$	$1\frac{4}{9}$	5
$2\frac{2}{5}$	$3\frac{3}{4}$	4	$4\frac{1}{6}$
$3\frac{2}{3}$	$7\frac{2}{5}$	$8\frac{1}{2}$	$4\frac{1}{4}$

Page 24

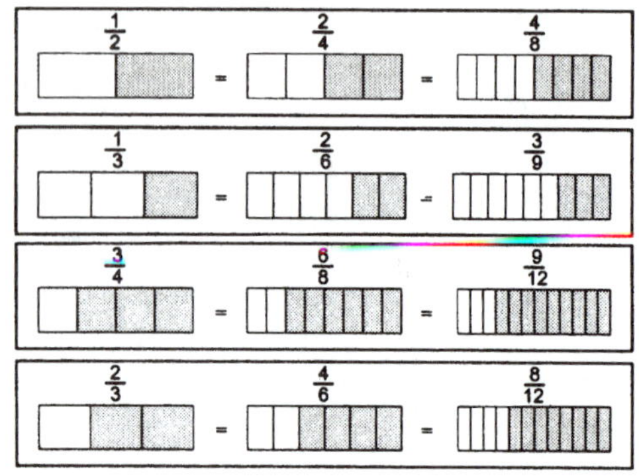

Page 25

$\frac{1}{3}\frac{\times 3}{\times 3} = \frac{3}{9}$	$\frac{1}{3}\frac{\times 4}{\times 4} = \frac{4}{12}$	$\frac{1}{4}\frac{\times 2}{\times 2} = \frac{2}{8}$
$\frac{1}{2}\frac{\times 4}{\times 4} = \frac{4}{8}$	$\frac{1}{6}\frac{\times 2}{\times 2} = \frac{2}{12}$	$\frac{1}{5}\frac{\times 3}{\times 3} = \frac{3}{15}$
$\frac{1}{8}\frac{\times 4}{\times 4} = \frac{4}{32}$	$\frac{1}{5}\frac{\times 6}{\times 6} = \frac{6}{30}$	$\frac{1}{7}\frac{\times 3}{\times 3} = \frac{3}{21}$
$\frac{2}{3}\frac{\times 3}{\times 3} = \frac{6}{9}$	$\frac{3}{8}\frac{\times 3}{\times 3} = \frac{9}{24}$	$\frac{4}{5}\frac{\times 4}{\times 4} = \frac{16}{20}$
$\frac{3}{7}\frac{\times 2}{\times 2} = \frac{6}{14}$	$\frac{2}{9}\frac{\times 2}{\times 2} = \frac{4}{18}$	$\frac{7}{8}\frac{\times 2}{\times 2} = \frac{14}{16}$
$\frac{5}{7}\frac{\times 3}{\times 3} = \frac{15}{21}$	$\frac{1}{6}\frac{\times 3}{\times 3} = \frac{3}{18}$	$\frac{7}{9}\frac{\times 3}{\times 3} = \frac{21}{27}$

Page 26

$\frac{1}{3}\frac{\times 2}{\times 2} = \frac{2}{6}$	$\frac{1}{3}\frac{\times 3}{\times 3} = \frac{3}{9}$	$\frac{1}{3}\frac{\times 12}{\times 12} = \frac{12}{36}$
$\frac{1}{2}\frac{\times 2}{\times 2} = \frac{2}{4}$	$\frac{1}{2}\frac{\times 3}{\times 3} = \frac{3}{6}$	$\frac{1}{2}\frac{\times 4}{\times 4} = \frac{4}{8}$
$\frac{1}{8}\frac{\times 3}{\times 3} = \frac{3}{24}$	$\frac{1}{5}\frac{\times 6}{\times 6} = \frac{6}{30}$	$\frac{1}{4}\frac{\times 3}{\times 3} = \frac{3}{12}$
$\frac{2}{3}\frac{\times 2}{\times 2} = \frac{4}{6}$	$\frac{3}{8}\frac{\times 2}{\times 2} = \frac{6}{16}$	$\frac{3}{5}\frac{\times 2}{\times 2} = \frac{6}{10}$
$\frac{2}{7}\frac{\times 2}{\times 2} = \frac{4}{14}$	$\frac{4}{9}\frac{\times 2}{\times 2} = \frac{8}{18}$	$\frac{5}{8}\frac{\times 2}{\times 2} = \frac{10}{16}$
$\frac{2}{3}\frac{\times 3}{\times 3} = \frac{6}{9}$	$\frac{3}{4}\frac{\times 3}{\times 3} = \frac{9}{12}$	$\frac{5}{6}\frac{\times 5}{\times 5} = \frac{25}{30}$
$\frac{2}{5}\frac{\times 2}{\times 2} = \frac{4}{10}$	$\frac{2}{5}\frac{\times 3}{\times 3} = \frac{6}{15}$	$\frac{2}{5}\frac{\times 4}{\times 4} = \frac{8}{20}$
$\frac{2}{9}\frac{\times 3}{\times 3} = \frac{6}{27}$	$\frac{1}{7}\frac{\times 3}{\times 3} = \frac{3}{21}$	$\frac{1}{9}\frac{\times 2}{\times 2} = \frac{2}{18}$
$\frac{3}{8}\frac{\times 3}{\times 3} = \frac{9}{24}$	$\frac{3}{8}\frac{\times 4}{\times 4} = \frac{12}{32}$	$\frac{4}{5}\frac{\times 4}{\times 4} = \frac{16}{20}$
$\frac{3}{7}\frac{\times 2}{\times 2} = \frac{6}{14}$	$\frac{2}{9}\frac{\times 2}{\times 2} = \frac{4}{18}$	$\frac{7}{8}\frac{\times 3}{\times 3} = \frac{21}{24}$

Page 27

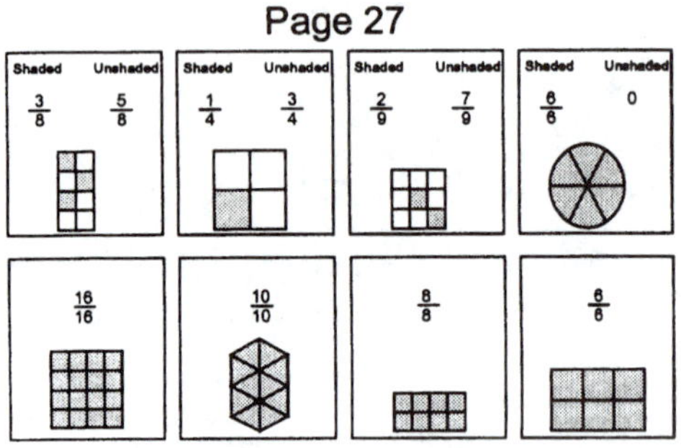

24	1	2	(3)	4	6	8	12	24		
21	1	(3)	7	21						
22	1	2	(11)	22						
33	1	3	(11)	33						
48	1	2	3	4	6	8	(12)	16	24	48
36	1	2	3	4	6	9	(12)	18	36	

$\frac{5}{23}$ $\frac{5}{19}$ $\frac{5}{9}$ $\frac{5}{7}$

$\frac{2}{11}$ $\frac{3}{11}$ $\frac{7}{11}$ $\frac{9}{11}$

Page 28

$\frac{2}{5}$	$\frac{6}{13}$	$\frac{1}{3}$
$\frac{4}{9}$	$\frac{1}{7}$	$\frac{3}{4}$
$\frac{1}{4}$	$\frac{2}{7}$	$\frac{11}{21}$

$\frac{9}{2}$ $\frac{27}{11}$ $\frac{53}{8}$

$9\frac{3}{8}$ $8\frac{1}{2}$ $3\frac{2}{3}$ $8\frac{2}{3}$

$\frac{2}{3}\frac{\times 3}{\times 3} = \frac{6}{9}$	$\frac{1}{9}\frac{\times 9}{\times 9} = \frac{9}{81}$	$\frac{3}{4}\frac{\times 2}{\times 2} = \frac{6}{8}$
$\frac{4}{5}\frac{\times 4}{\times 4} = \frac{16}{20}$	$\frac{5}{6}\frac{\times 3}{\times 3} = \frac{15}{18}$	$\frac{3}{11}\frac{\times 6}{\times 6} = \frac{18}{66}$
$\frac{3}{7}\frac{\times 4}{\times 4} = \frac{12}{28}$	$\frac{4}{9}\frac{\times 3}{\times 3} = \frac{12}{27}$	$\frac{2}{7}\frac{\times 3}{\times 3} = \frac{6}{21}$